Unable Mother

Helen Calcutt

V.

Published in the United Kingdom in 2018
by V. Press,
10 Vernon Grove,
Droitwich,
Worcestershire,
WR9 9LQ.

ISBN: 978-1-9998444-0-0

Cover image 'Retreat' © Katherine Sheers, 2017

Cover design © Ruth Stacey, 2018

Printed in the U.K. by Imprint Digital, Seychelles Farm, Upton Pyne, Exeter EX5 5HY, on recycled paper stock.

Acknowledgements

Thank you to the editors of the following publications in which some of these poems first appeared: *ENVOI, Poetry Scotland, Poetry Wales, New Welsh Review, The London Magazine, The Brooklyn Review, Equinox, The Offi Press, Ink Sweat & Tears.*

With love and thanks to my dear family, friends, and advisers (poetic, spiritual or otherwise) especially, Mario Petrucci, Greta Stoddart, Paul Henry, Gary Raymond, Robert Peake, John Beynon, Zoe Davies, Anna Russell, Kerry Featherstone, Jonathan Davidson, Spike Barker, David Calcutt (Dad) Sue Calcutt (Mom) Peter Tinkler, Sasha Dugdale, Ted Hughes, Janos Pilinszky, Alice Walker, Emily Berry, Glyn Hughes, Anne Sexton, Vasko Popa, Tomas Transtromer, Alice Oswald.

Deepest thanks to my inspiration, and muse; Josephene.

This book is in memory of my brother, Matthew.

V.

Contents

Pale disturbance 7

God 9

White almond 11

Something 13

Dissolving 14

Turbulence comes in the form of birds 17

Bird 18

Melon Picker 19

North Light 21

Teeth 22

Orphan mother 23

The Gardener 24

Crossing 26

Stable dawn 27

Hibernation season 29

Unable mother 30

Flesh 32

Hurt 34

To be young, to grow... 35

"This entrance closes at dusk" 38

Hours 40

Bureau 41

Song for a man who sleeps 42

Now I have touched the dark water 43

Josephene (and the crickets) 44

The listening tree 45

Driving 47

To the ruins 48

Ruins 49

Fish 50

V.

Tremor   51
Tremor   52
Lovesong to One child   53
Anvil   54
Inferno glass   55
Naked   57
If you watch the sky moving backwards   58

V.

'And over time, more pale, more ignorant.
Silent, like wingbeats,
heavy, and ignorant.'

V.

From 'Unable Mother 1/I' –
an unfinished poem whose trace threads
through this whole collection.

V.

Pale disturbance

First comes the feeling.
The fraying of light,
before a feeling
of falling.

Their edges
        incline like ears,
listening,
their small mouths
talking

such tender forms
of ubiquitous light,
tickling in from all sides,

spreading, as cancer might
behind the eyes
where your vision is holed,

where your future
and intimate dreamings are stored
now gaining to a field.

Where these sparks,
these pollen wheels
of broken dusk

blow your secrets to the bush,
like embers cupped
from dishes of ash,

they're let go now
with the blanket wind,
pale and wild

with the reflection of your skin;

where it slides
a slow river into light,
you progress, with these driftings

from window-watcher
to 'flight'.

God

You planted a single yellow tulip.
How it grew, you couldn't say.
Perhaps it winged

a little wordless, perhaps it tried
a lit chord
and then yellow

as the suckle of sleep, as a child warms
to the yolk of a breast,
it warmed to the air it repeated.

It comes back, year on year.
The pleasure of the ghost
is that it grows to learn

how achingly it can pass through walls,
through time,
like a golden ring, it can shine

but never be touched.
I remember
how I looked at my mother's

knot – when she slipped her finger
through the round and the cold
and said 'no

it belongs here.'
I never feared
a thing I couldn't have.

Even when I sit in the shadows
of the house
and the trees are looping through

with not a single path that's lit to see you –

it's the promise of what you are,
what you will become.

White almond

We fit near perfect.
Pulling the invisible ring
over the shape of our mouths.

Widening at the shoulders,
a consistency of skins,
where sweat

takes a thin
route,
from the nape of the neck

to the bow-spine.
Floating coccyx
flung

wide open –
I fall
from my flesh into his

and what stings
clutches at lily brains,
pulses,

everywhere white.
We feed
on the apex flower's

root. My cunt
is blown cochineal.
I throw my arms to the sun,

and my twenty-odd years
fall away with old
lungs,

old way-of-doing-things

heart.
He knows love

is meant to live on in the body.
Open-kissed, he presses
an almond between my breasts,

already growing a remarkable sweetness.
Coming away,
I dream of thickets,

pale river-streams
and crickets.
My flesh making heaven of it.

Something

is realising itself,
in the corner of my eye.
Discovering a form.
Near-absolute, though tenuous
in flesh,
two hollowed wings blown one,
and leaning backwards into the light.

It purrs, and wakes wet.
Wants to dry itself
on my fall-away clothes,
nuzzle in, and suck
my skin
a little harder.

And then there's this
colour. Something
like blue
that's been fading with time
spreads through me like
winter sands

as if I could purify it.
Maybe I can.

Dissolving

for mom and me

slippery womb where
tiny arms and legs
hollowed like sugar

and the empty space
beneath her daughter
wholly insisted

•

and then terribly/
beautifully

•

trying to resolve
the sifting of worlds
escaping beneath her

•

just cool enough
for there to have been light
for feet to have curled
for blood to have passed
for cells to drain
through one single
extraordinary   opening

•

shrinking from the womb gate

•

receding down
from the womb

if   wombs
were the musk and smell

of crumbling light

it vanished   into it

•

no   parting of thighs
no   blood

or trickles of water

the tissues they said *were simply absorbed*

like a droning sound

or a white

                  gull

                        crossing

•

it's too simple she says

can your body
make something
die afresh?

can you atone the loss
of something
you hardly had at all?

•

No.

Though it flickers
somewhere in the mind.
Shadows behind the eyes.

Turbulence comes in the form of birds

trying to balance the air
as wind and life rolls through them –

unfolding, like magic, their flyaway selves
are exposed, and made free.

It's beautiful, watching the vulnerable.
How they glide and play

among their own soft shadows,
net-catching the light

that could at any moment split;
at once a darkness, and a wet day,

a dry eye – and a drumwheel of feathers.
There was this one

we tried to save. It fell, like a broken wheel,
into our garden.

It rolled into my body,
because I was wide, and open to it.

I tried to walk with it,
I couldn't turn. I tried to run

but the wheel
crushed the meat-flower of my heart.

It was only when I stopped

and there was blood

that I realised it was a bird.

Bird

for Noah

Lamp in paperfields
and in the sky, a compression of long halls.

Do you know how sudden you are
how sad? Sadness being air
or soft fly of a thing
over dark houses.

The sad dying voice of the bird
is my dying voice.

We are the poem – look
our heads, tongues
drag with the old clock.

This is how it has to be.
The shadows dancing on the eaves
know our trick

of being one thing.
Bird,

when you lower the lamp
of your voice,
my mouth rises to its light,
I dilate under your finger-tones.

If you fall, the moon
will step down
and hold you close.

Melon Picker

Death touched your feet
with its wing.

It felt
how you cut the cord, carried
their boulder warmth

from the lip of the leaf
to the gut of the bowl.

Every time the wind
disturbed a shock of trees,
the dry light

eclipsed your vision.
You would drop them,

drag them. Could I ever
understand the pain
of broken feet? Where you knelt

under the night's drunken expanse,
bleeding the lines

you walked, you wept...
sheer tiredness
was the thing that killed us

as it killed you then.
Seeing the same sun

bloat gold,
over black boulder seeds,
knocking like enormous breasts.

To greet the toll
that carried the dawn,

lifting your song-lines
and you
back, to the barren harvest.

North Light

There was a marbled absence.
The helmeted snow in the yard
held its iron,
water honeyed

in the slung bucket
where the sun stooped
like a small lamp
cooling against the grey wall

of each thinning afternoon.
So my hands have broken
on your neck, and mouth –
our whitening stone

has gathered dust, and the air
dithers where we talk
in a corner of light
by the small window.

Now you turn from the window
with your book, and lamp.
Now you sit, empty-lapped
with absent hands

and a lustreless mouth –
and here is a space,
again, our pale sky rising
at the tick of two clocks.

And here is love
like a pale sheet, sunk
against the pale earth.

Teeth

From a blindfold of lips,
every particular touch
is as hurting is to grass.

On these nights, your fingers
almost sensibly
set their task to air –

almost regrettably tease the lotus
notion of passing, not
skin to skin

or such heat,
but taking a route
rendering the half-opened flower of the mouth

something harder,
sweeter.
Only moments at a time

does the singing note
of my spine
rise organically;

rise again
like a snake between the eyes –
so you are fortunate

to graze the map of my thigh
but sink hard in the head.
Make a woman

instead of some
lying leaf. Or totem of grief.

Orphan mother

She gave her to you. She died
and you opened yourself out,
the bleeding heart of
mother.
They died, didn't they? Both.
It happened in a single blow
of hot life to the body,
after so much rain.

And how still, always. The soundless
purpled stretch of sky
over an endless sand,
or the glass of a hand
when a brain drops to stillness
(I know this from experience)

never mind the moon,

you have offered yourself out
the heaviest breathing
lotus flower,
opened a blooming wound.
You have control.
And in all this world,
did you think

you could ever
come back? Mother of face, conceive
of a chance to darn
her purpled lace.
Make all this right again?
Give her dead mother's rooms
a little light again?

The Gardener

I go to him when the lakes are quiet,
when blossom holds its breath
in bluest south.
The horses

have strung up their miles
and collect inwards towards the light –
coal,
and all the dim world's glow,

this earth-meal and dust
now damp
and glittering in this autumn's constant.
All the flames that go up

are a mortal shout.
The gardener's burn,
its heat and grain

reveal him in his awfulness
tending the ruined mass,
this mode of a man
I've learned to love

tackles leaf, and loom, drags
the swollen bosom of wood
from a belly of wire

and bluish thistle.
He wants it all to burn.
We drain the lakes,
their glass up-sends in fume,

their iris codes
flurry, and whiten the air
to our killing conditions –

in this blood-red insistence
committing ourselves.
The horses walk on
like women through fire.

Crossing

This stable feels like a boat. Its roof rocks the hollow.
There are windows on every side,
concealed. Though it feels
like a heart exposed,
if hearts are water.
There are horses hanging like oars.
The darkest pool touches at their eyes,
where their small lives are suspended.
My hands are trembling.
I imagine they're wings,
that my mind could navigate
the darkest crossing.
If crossings were these waters, or a drowning field.

And by field, I mean
the resting place of my daughter.
The animal world that keeps her,
before I wake her.

Stable dawn

When the first word of the sun has lifted,
and given her name –

I go to the stables. Dark,
and plumy, though there are no birds.

I feel for her
as the beasts materialise.

Forms within shape
and stone

among bookcases of dark heat,
like mouths held wide

feeling outwards for the lint sun –
as if its light sleeps

beneath them all. They ache and creak
over the rotation of its ball

that, for now, holds them still.
As if they'd been going all night

over the moonshape of the earth,
they doze and snort, their heads

hang like gods
with the very weight of it.

That yes, they're a mortal kind.
That a second world of darkness climbs

to make shadows of their bones.
And I,
some life-seeker

am   pulled,
a hoofish tide. There's one here

who's mine to guide,
and what she guards

featureless,
I'll gather up in silence.

To fling open these doors, and stride.
To bound,

to flood – straight on
from the stable

eye,
into the living world.

Hibernation season

Time has swept armour
under my skin.
By flakes, by moments.

I resist
that I'm entered.
No hush from the door

softly, where feet tread
I feel no weight in the room,
though something in me comes –

and comes again,
daily.
The seasonal murmur

of her body
rounding its warm glass,
then something like a hand

the iridescence of woken fingers –
I want to know them
but can't. Though my womb has showed

there's armour and
flesh division – such collisions
of shaking light –

there should be gold in my bed,
her name
should fill the blank

theatre of my head.
Where her season might always be dead.

Unable mother

I hide, yet I open my mouth to the light –
I hurt
the people I love. It's not love
when grace from the body
falls,
to leave grace and light
all over the floor.

I shed. I am made of lines,
I am colourless.
I am trying
to bury a life –
I am trying to grow it.
It's like squeezing
the flesh and fruit of the mind
to a single drop of light.

This is the effort.
Without moving,
you scoop and gather
and scoop and gather
what's meek and tender.
I'm unable to feel
I'm creating a daughter.
In my head,
this thing is a boy,

it sits on a throne,
and like a thrush sings
about the spittle of its bones.
It's like squeezing
flesh and fruit from the bone,
this terrible love.
And I can speak

as if the act of growing is done
but there are little stamps of blood.
I panic – in my body, I am
giving back his blood.
It was me, I couldn't stop her from
dancing on his blood.

Flesh

can't fathom the words,

though your skin
might
from time to time

recover a scent,
a world away
in rhythms

of white walls,
where moons are tugged down,
and shame

is the only principle.
O, to be so
openly naked,

how to account for that?
So much of you
was sunk,

a sack in a bed
fisting down the screams,
numb

to the vital wave of vibrations –
despite the pressures
they applied,

to open you out,
your abilities failed.
You couldn't accept

the natural
give,   the heavy
flower

of your uterus,
someone had to drug
every knot in your spine,

so you could hide
beyond the yellow mask of sleep;

almost in death,
as the contractions in you crept

ever lower
with the infant's head –

at her deepest point,
the shadow-doctors
pulled her gory from the womb.

Despite the glorious
pools of blood, you insisted

you felt nothing.
Even when the last
toe

slipped hard
and white
from the vertical wound...

you couldn't mouth the sounds.
Your innards,
like a blown flower,

totally emptied.

O, to be so
openly naked.
How to account for that?

Hurt

What if I hadn't brought you
into this world?
Would it have been kinder to abort

the hurting in its sack,
that only comes with a birth,
and everything after its blood.

The frustrations of love,
they lie,
they wait like

lily-pads
on globes of water. It only takes
a briar of touch,

and their shape unfolds,
stemming wide for a branch,
both in darkness and sun.

And these ripples, they slow to define
these utter depths of love,
as how rushed, and how sudden in the eye

when it wells this wild –

and your pools, they're the great
tears in the universe. The holy gaps
I consider and see

a delicate god. And that she's
unrefined, reaching out, like that lily,
like   the first careful coming of the mind,

awareness and fearfulness
all at once, from the mind.
Desperate for me to be kind.

To be young, to grow, and learn the hardest lesson from your neighbour

How
in years to come
she will wander into the same
garden

and nothing
will be the same,

though everything will be lit
   and inclining towards

                    like a woman in the rush

          floating backwards – her ribs and neck

floating backwards for that light –

to remember in their lucidity
the years' fruitful complexity,

the times that were,
the moments
she stepped forwards

and stepped again
into the still and gold,
the enchantments that formed,

made her pause (again)
for the will of the garden.

And knowing you, as she did,
a second father to the first,

knowing me, as I am,
the one who urged her

under those globes,
those infinite, summer-patch worlds

where the sun fell
                    just-so,

those gaps
were a torch for your
love

to light under,

and yes, how she grows,
how it hurts to see her now

having grown to believe
what a garden contains – that greens are souls,
and that souls are often bent
to return.

She learns

          the patient game of love

and in years to come, she will recall – "this
is how we burn"

and the night will scratch
     with a giving of stars,

                    falling across her like a thread

                              bright and instant as a blow
to the head –

just as you
would have said, "wait your turn,"
she will cry at the hour

and then pause for the sound
to sink.
The leaves will letter you

leaf, by link.

Make your going the very same

as growing a grief or path of skin.

"This entrance closes at dusk"

for Dad

And beyond the iron, a map of veins.
Veins, that are branches,
run like coal. They burn
part orange, under the weight of the sun.

Near as touch, and as real
as your lung
reaching golden from the mind,
and, in times like these, when the sky

is a fit of orange in the breeze,
they gather at the roof of a wood.
You recall
how this burns. You know

how to breathe, how to feel
under the collapse of the light,
when hours are drawn and nearing their pass –

though not aged, nor afeard.
Even miles on the road (when the wood
isn't near) you remember
how to run backwards into that world – when light

and leaf-roots slip
under your nerves (much like rain
tickling the roof of a cloud)
even from lovers you're drawn, like a flag,

to that fire. Like balloons, or children
floating to the spire –
the very ring-spine of dreams,

which is a tree

winding a night-song to call

                              other trees...

They're all touching in the breeze.
And those distinctive shapes
may be round, in the dark, may be bent,

but all those mouths tilting up,
all the gazing and the wonder,
such rare, secluded openness –

they're all living and dreaming a realer moment,
they have nothing to lose at all.
There's nothing more serious, or golden,
or God,

beyond the gates, after dusk.

Hours

Our good hours
span like days. Rotate
like hands of water

turning like minds,
under glass, openly seen.
Openly brave and seeking.

Searching the clear
crystal mind
for the fruits of glass.

Those curved, honest,
moony
                    transparences

of unfickled love. Unspoiled
unstained, untinctured
love –

like an opening into the glove
of the heart,
bled of velvet.

We dream these hours,
we live them. We cocoon
and case our daughter inside them.

We play on them with spoons; a tinkering sound.
When the hours are good,
it draws her out.

Bureau

What did you see from where you whispered?
Where your shadow gains tread
on the roof of the floor,

disturbance
has leaked through, many times,
discovered it can make music;

the blow of a hand
to a head for instance,
or what must have been a broken mouth.

What they heard, down there,
you saw. I see you have
two holes, that a key

or tooth might unlock,
much like these holes above my hip
where the wings split.

I wasn't trying to fly.
I can't remember
how the light touched me,

or if my eyes were closed.
When I stop to think, I see her face,
though I can't remember the room,

if you were there at all,
if she covered her face with her hands,
or was glowing, like a moon.

Song for a man who sleeps

Where there's time passing,
there's every moment
a death.
Though I could swim
the narrow escape of this bed,
there's worship in my head.

Worship of a dream
inside the ear,
that's in darkness. A tenderness
that's very old,
a gift, that in this sleeping calls
through tangled reeds,

where light blows from a gap in the sea,

that is a moon at hand.

Where his face and mouth
are made sore by the moon,
he offers me love.
Even when our love
closes its fingers to constrict,
there is salt upon our lips.

As if the sea had bled
with borrowed life, when there is none of it.

Now I have touched the dark water

the moon sways to her lamp,
the light is heavy, and warm
and overcome

with a lifting of grief,
a lightness of moonlight –
heady, indifferent to the swing

of the sea
which hangs low,

which too is a lamp
which too is lifted
entirely from grief

which is full and emptied of grief –

grief, pushed out like a small boat
after the moon –
grief, which hovers between sea and sky,

lamp and mind

grief,
held out, and held long
through winds

in the act of trying to sing,
is tired, lets go.
Lays down like a child

with its feet to the oars,

mouth to the world.

Josephene (and the crickets)

Your head is a gift, which
when I lower to touch,
ruminates the various
places you've been,
the places you haven't.

And yet there's a sense of them
there, of where we'll be,
ringing a coastline
of dust on the screen
of light,

above your head, much like the haze that crowns
the stones of the dead.

Though you're very much alive,
and tapping
at earth's flint,

like summer crickets
in their sun-robes, in heat,

in the whisper of all these things...

we collect our desires
like a bucket of rings   *(sing)*

to earn us wings.

The listening tree

I don't know when this began. I have an ear
for the beautiful/terrible
sounds, soaked with rain.
With my hearing in such leaves,
I can bear the worst of human music.
I've gone so very far, listening
without moving. My roots are bound
by ribbons in the earth
which lengthen into my back
and I sway, as it happens
in these roots from my back. I listen,
and sleep between the dark
and the dark
where my hearing is suspended.
And between this and my skull,
it's all dark matter,
where earth and her sweetness
have darkened to gather each
bone to a bone,
every coil to a chord.
I sing, though you wouldn't know it.
My mouth is sunk in a pool
of old life,
it glitters and tries
to sing of its light,
and cries owl-cries
for a secret way out. Still, I bend
my thick spine
to bare my neck, and touch you.
You could almost be a stranger
who's found me by a road,
you hold out your arms
as if you hold the great world,
you place your hands
on my body and hair. Your tears
catch on the quiet in the air,

and shake and glitter with the shakings
of your hair;
something in your shape
is like a tree, like me. I barely brush you
and your mouth comes alive on my light,
I barely sigh I am a temple, I am
soaking you with light.
If I could birth myself a second time,
I'd have your soul.
You rock and sigh 'oh I'm done, Mother,
I'm done.' But the young, my love,
are free, or didn't you know? There's no
god in this world.
The closest thing to prayer is
a child who says she hurts.

Driving

Nees Kydonies, Greece

I hold you as I was held.
We go as I went.
Through dark, as it aspires again
to the light. It reaches and turns

its face to the hills,
the silk of its arms
to the spread of its hands.
And spills a love, that lifts

from under stones,
that's spoken of in the hills.
That speaks as we slip
like purgatory birds,

and deeply;
it tells there's almost always a road out,
and of looking to the blue,
where the sea is moving

as I'm moving with you,
as we're warm, and everything
smells of the light,
we're safe, my darling, with soakings of light.

We are directionless, but definitely
leaving things behind. The stones are sweet
as they're kicked to the side
and we continue to drive –

are you my mother, am I mine,
are we nameless for a time,
with this lightness in our spines
peaceful for a time?

To the ruins

I strode through the long white grass
with my long white thighs.
I found the summit beneath my feet, I found

the total expanse of my love
in the long lifting neck of the sea.
I felt it hang there, like feeling

in suspense. I felt the long grass shiver,
and the white sun flex;
I followed where your shadow

fixed its blade over the grass.
Blunt like a wilderness,
it flexed and begged a brighter wilderness.

I watched the sun meet with your eye
like a huge bird – it landed on your shoulders
and cried "this way! this way!"

I followed, I swayed
in the long grass. Let it touch
                    at my hips
                              like *this;*
I didn't mind
that it itched, or the fine, seizured cuts
(like the peckings of a small, dangerous foot)

– my shadow writhed, like an alligator,
in the heat, from a nest.
It splayed exquisite throats of the grass,

and I thought
if this is only walking
(if this is only walking...)

Ruins

Thermi, Greece

There are poppies everywhere. A handful of heat
to scatter over their dead
heads,
their pretty shoulders.

And mine too. My shadow has fallen
over the drapery of stones,
I hear its call,

bent heavy by the wind,
on singing the wind's song.

It streams, like a deep tide, through my cockled
ear.
It tells me

this world is old. That time and I
have collapsed on these shores.
That waiting is done.
That this ruinous, poppied place is home.

Fish

Go swim with her. She is happy
for you to learn
the way of her skin

when it is wet,
or the look of her head
as it cleaves the syrup of water,

and drenches the arid sun
when climbing out
all sudden, all dark –

and the stones, they will sing
dark
with the impressions of you.

Air hangs wide
with the rush of where you've been,
as you come clean

of all the things you've done,
the many ways
you've abused one another.

You talk and talk (the endless chatter)
and then, quiet,
sink

like a hollowing of fish,
hollow matter.
Remember this, when you lie in bed,

when doubt kisses
the gilt of your head –
and you wind tight like a thread.

Tremor

Were there two? Each inclined

towards the other,

and the other's

self

Inclined to slow, in the blood, to do
a servant's work,

to die, almost,
but peel away laughing
like so
                many

                        stars...

knocking their knuckles and fortunes on the air –
we've lived, we've glitched!
we tremor
in the ditch!

and doing what has to be done
to give so much light but

light as little as possible

the pathway to knowing

Just an empty field
and a few lights blowing

Tremor

Nothing speaks until all's gone quiet
and you're domestic and cold,
domestic and warm.

Hanging washing by the window, and then
the sun comes in a splash from under a cloud,
and the moon is starched paper.

You see your own flesh, your own eyes,
your very own dormant, ringing   silence

coming alive and then awake,

like clouds unfolding their skins over the lake,
undoing all things that were done.
To take and take,

and give and give

the last pain seen,
the last word heard,
the last moment felt.

Lovesong to One child

I will watch your face unfold
like the surface of the moon.
I will hear idiots talking,
and only acknowledge
the coral

hollow of your ear,
the passing of breath,
through every passage you exhale
your shadows' soft-
hooded weariness.

The window has all
but escaped us here. Like its murmuring haze,
your lungs cocoon
our quiet in a shroud,
like the deep groan
of a listening drum –

our shadows will become
vocal, they will say
they want to be with you.
They want to feel
what it is to speak the dark,
without ever saying a word.

Anvil

for the one unborn

It quietened the night you died
going back

into the blow of the smite
that buried you like winter.

In my bed,
skin-clots furred.
Blood

climbed
throat, and lip. My mother's shadow
danced on the wall.

And you,
child, sensing

your fore-shield above,
set your glow
on my motherhood step.
Fostered and re-fostered the light.

Inferno glass

All I can say is   *glass*
though it was flesh that touched
and changed me.

I have to say that when you
touched me that time,
it wasn't kind.

I can't find the words
for the rest,
all I can think of is

glass

shattered or shut,
opened out, or a sheet,
or a particle-field of glass

beneath our feet,

or a glass mind working.

I press my mouth under it,
and scream.
It creates air and oddities

of light and steam –

how can this be?
– eventless smoke to flicker, and bleed...

I see myself, I write it.
You may want me to write
the flesh and blood of it,

but anyhow,

I didn't bleed, and going on,
there's always more to it than there seems....

I press my mouth under it,
and scream.
And if I'm right, living this way

is like a dream
or the suffix of a dream   *very cold.*

And in this way
I'm like Ariel. Burning in the cold.

Naked

Skin is woman. Light is hard
and keen on her back
as she lowers to undress.

Or does she dress naked?
Unfold her many
doubted selves

under the blaze of the moon.
Naked that is night. Two hands
withdraw from the pulsing lamp

that could circle the room,
like a watch, like time,
coined into the river of her back.

She will never be old. Every move
to undress
is to dress again, openly

and by the gaze of the world:
a wing, and then an eye
a window into the night.

She will never be old.
The still and calm
interior of her self – as you might see –

is heavenly and dark.
Reaching naked through the glass,
a kind of light.

If you watch the sky moving backwards

really keep your eyes on it

you can become its sense of space and light
                              You might fall
a second time out of love
float wide and loveless so very easily

This sense of
not knowing who you are

can become the way you want to be
in the absence of ghosts
there's no mind
you can put to remembering   Only listening
of a sort   far and near
to the thrum of the world
where it bucks and slides   or flies
like your feet
either side   or ahead of you

attentive to fear perhaps
though un-lifting
where light throws its skins for a hoodless star –
or a gossamer field
lit wide not dark

not heaven not light

you can see yourself as no-one
to the world
no-one reflected
you will be surprised in the relief
of having removed yourself completely

simply nothing
to the sky   or to you   And all that is blue
to us and awake

can be absent and awake
bright-eyed yet asleep

HELEN CALCUTT is a globally published poet and critic. Her work features in over forty journals, and she performs her work internationally. She has taken on writing residences with The National Trust and Loughborough University, where she is also a visiting lecturer in Creative and Professional Writing.

Helen's pamphlet collection, *Sudden rainfall*, was published by experimental publishing house Perdika Press when she was just 23 years old. It was shortlisted for the PBS Pamphlet Choice award and became a Waterstones' best-selling collection in 2016. *Unable Mother* is her first full-length book of poems.

V.